Muskox & Goat Songs

Muskox

&

Goat Songs

Olga Costopoulos

Ekstasis Editions

Canadian Cataloguing in Publication Data

Costopoulos, Olga
  Muskox & goat songs.

Poems.
ISBN 0-921215-88-6

I. Title.
PS8555.087M87 1995 C811'.54   C95-910224-8
PR9199.3.C67M87 1995

© Olga Costopoulos, 1995
Cover art: Noreen Tomlinson, "Anniversary", 1994

Acknowledgements

The Antigonish Review, ARC, Contemporary Verse II, Dandelion, The Fiddlehead, Grasslands Review, Light: A Quarterly of Light Verse, Negative Capability, The New Quarterly, NeWest Review, Nimrod. Some of the poems were broadcast on CBC's *Alberta Anthology*.

The author gratefully acknowledges a grant from the Alberta Foundation for the Arts which permitted the preparation of this manuscript.

Published in 1995 by
Ekstasis Editions Canada Ltd.   **Ekstasis Editions**
Box 8474, Main Postal Outlet   Box 571
Victoria, B.C. V8W 3S1   Banff, Alberta T0L 0C0

Muskox & Goat Songs has been published with the assistance of the Canada Council and the Cultural Services Branch of British Columbia.

Printed and bound in Canada by Hignell Printing, Winnipeg, Manitoba.

Contents

for Bert, Meli and Vasilis

The Muskox Poems

Horn Envy

Marvel at the muskox
magnificently furred
ivory tiara always in place
ankles delicate
on hooves of polished slate
grazing like dieting dowagers
on the lean cuisine of arctic grasses
leisured, deliberate,
ruminating on the world
from near its top
content but never complacent
knowing that the hair that keeps
the calving belly warm
is the finest in the world
and softer than any down
those bosomy geese can produce.

Omingmang Nivorpok

If I believed in an afterlife
I'd imagine Keats paused in fancy's flight
on some low-flying cloud to contemplate
this prairie airport, a glass vitrine
containing another paradox
of motion suspended. He might notice
another a bit like him, standing rapt
in front of another glass case
fingering the letters on the brazen plaque,
marvelling, mouthing, whispering the words
to feel their sounds—and feel again

Omingmang Nivorpok: the tongue contorts
around the strange Inuit sounds
sounds like the high Arctic wind whining
sidewise over the snow——and then
a hoofsound poking—pok—
through a crust of ice.

Omingmang Nivorpok.
It means, "big hairy one worries."
The cows and bulls are one, a circle
of carven solidarity in stone

The calves are separate pieces
in heedless play inside their round corral—
a ring of shaggy butts and instinct.
The young will never know they were formed
from the same soft stone as their elders,
but smaller, more frangible,
never know of the wolves whose ivory fangs
long for their silken flanks.

A romantic might imagine this herd
was carved by a husband and wife—
he chipping out the shapes
she combing stone into hair
that seems to ripple in a wind
both chiselling out and sharpening
hooves to raise against the craven wolf
set snarling in each corner of the glass.

"I am the muskox"

No, I am not the walrus, gurgling, jubilant
afloat on a glassy sea
I am the muskox and I walk upon the earth
pawing my living from beneath the snow
No, I am not the snow goose buffeted,
blown by the northwind to some southern shore
I am the muskox and I face the winds
though they make mischief in my skirt of hair
No, I am not the wolverine with fierce teeth
who cannot bear company even of his own kind
I am the muskox and I love my herd
for they too are companionable beasts
No, I am not the wolf with yellow eyes
who stares and would stalk my children
I am the muskox and I know my enemy
I am not man--

Advanced Courtship

The male muskox, writes the zoologist,
carries his head in a certain way
when approaching a receptive female—
higher than usual, steady,
not swinging from side to side with each footfall.
The term is "a walk with intent."
You vary your gait as well,
grazing the aisles of bookstores
you barely move, your head bent.
Then there's the nervous stationary shift
from foot to foot in a dress shop,
arms folded, eyes glazed, irrepressible yawns,
and I know you walk among strangers—
a shy toeing-out, as if on snowshoes,
as if you fear breaking through
the veneers whose thinness you can always smell.
My favourite, the one I cannot see but feel,
is your stride up the stairs, behind me.
Your best walk. Your best intent.

The Death of the Muskox

The field zoologist reported that
the oldest bull just wandered away
abandoning the herd, not driven off
by any younger challenger
eager to breed and beget.
He simply walked away
not in pursuit of pleasure
nor in flight from pain—but drawn
by the weakening tide of his blood
to the edge of his world
where even the wolves
waited upon his dignity
for three days, three nights,
until his shuddering,
slobbering
end.

The zoologist, whose vigil
lacked the constancy of the wolves'
didn't quite make the funereal feast.
By the time he arrived
these northern gods
had claimed as theirs
the still-warm entrails
and his axe was no match
for the wolves' strong jaws.
Unable to carve out a stiff-frozen leg
to examine its bone marrow cells—
he collected a few pellets
then made his way back to camp
reflecting upon the nature
of predation.

Stubborn Memory in Stubborn Root

Migraine/Buzz Saw

It was always called the buzz-saw
used only in the autumn to cut
the winter's worth of wood.
This ritual transubstantiation
from tree to log to flame to warm
was performed only by the menfolk.
Children never needed to be sent away
from the peril of flying chips and knots.
They hid from its hissing scream by instinct,
in the furthest corner of the farmhouse.
The mother could not hide, nor show
her fear as she carried water past.
Nerves those days were serrated too.
Grooves appeared in the woman's forehead
but no one noticed. Later the neighbours
would argue whether or not she knew
what she was about when she walked
into the blade, smiling, saying to herself,
There now, maybe I'll be able to do twice the work.

Birds and Beasts

Her tongue is thick, coated
immovable, bloated.
She might as well
be Philomel.

She'd kept a hoard of polished pebbles
called them her herd. Her own rock cows.
Like her, obedient, they never breached
the round corrals she wove for them
from oat straw yellow as her long straight hair.
She watched and sang to them
warmed their calves in her hand

Later, she would fling the herd away
picking them up by the handful
mixed with bits of the grass
they could not eat,
hurling them at her older brothers
with all her ineffectual rage.
Then she moved indoors. For good.

She started to play the piano.
She learned that only the innocent
could play at play. Opposites changed positions.
The opposite of play is not work
but guilt and shame unspeakable.

She worked the keys and pedals
beyond, outside the circle of the dance.
Knowledge, visceral, carnal,
set her upon the stage
but she could never sing.

She knows now Yeats was not quite right.
Leda's knowledge was her power.
And rape breeds indifference in no one:
she also knows why the swan can sing
only when it is ready to die.

Piano Forte

We are always either fleeing pain or pursuing pleasure.
Al-Farabi

The piano came into our house by force
of several sweating, swearing men
who had to remove the door frame
to admit the Trojan horse of art
Had they but known how soon
how completely they would lose me to it
they'd have saved their time and energy

When it came in through that ragged door
I couldn't see the keys, didn't know
they were covered up, protected
waiting for me to open them
let them open for me
a world worlds away, reachable
by a twirl of the clawfooted stool

Instrument, altar, haven of sound—
proof of where I was, that I was
My cleverest trick was being there
visible, playing, yet coaxing out
my legion notes, arrows sent singing
into barbarian hearts
all the while out of reach
of hectoring reality

Daughters of Wisdom

I

More than the pain itself I remember
the evening, the taunting, the fall.
The evening—July, calves and children
playing late with growing shadows
My brother, twelve, saying "Chickenshit girl."
The corral seeming vast, the fattening steers
My own long time deciding—

It happened so quickly—
The steer in the chute, raging
Me gripping his round sides with bony knees
and then, the jerk of motion.
My fall was quick, into the muck.
The steer kicked out in panic,
to wrist, elbow, shoulder.

I hadn't heard about shock yet
but later that summer, home from hospital,
I tried to climb the corral fence
using only my left arm. I couldn't.

II

The ride into town was long and rough
and I could not stop shivering.
I smelled like cow manure.
The hospital was the biggest building
I had ever seen—brick, white and pillared.
The sombre nun in the admitting room
rose from her desk, tall as my father
and even his voice softened for her.
When she asked, "Catholic or Protestant?"
the usual pride of his "I ain't nuthin" was gone.
He'd even removed his hat.

III

The x-ray technician, Sister Anne,
wheeled me into a cold bright room
and smiled to reassure me.
"This may cause some discomfort," she said
then straightened out my green-stick fractured arm.
I clenched the other fist and wouldn't cry,
said nothing till a second splinter of bone
broke through the skin, and with it, blood—
a heathen spatter on her starched white wimple.
I whispered I was sorry.

She explained how x-rays worked their magic
of looking at people inside.
I'd heard of Catholics and confession—
was this how they found out your sins?

IV

In traction, from my cool clean bed
I'd watch the sisters go about their work.
Their motion was more like flight.
They scarcely seemed to touch the floor.
I came to call them angels.
Familiar, I one day asked a nun
if they really flew, or went on roller skates.
Laughing, she revealed her slippered feet.

V

Proud as I was of my stiff white cast—
I imagined it made of old wimples—
I had no desire to leave this new home
and return to my former life.
The hospital rooms had been so clean,
no cracks in the curtained windows,
and the breeze that blew in
brought roses and peonies, not cow dung.
And my brother seemed larger, coarser,
yet somehow less a threat to me.
Perhaps he felt that my index finger,
extended, stiff from a damaged nerve,
was pointing in his direction.

I looked for more of the whiteness
I'd grown to love so much.
Sheets at home were rough greyed flannel
and smelled of too many unwashed bodies.

One day, while hiding in the coal cellar,
I saw among the great black lumps
one that startled me with its shape.
It had no white, but the glossy form
was shaped like a seated nun.
Even the family agreed
we shouldn't burn it.

She sat for years on my windowsill,
neither art nor icon, but solid
bituminous metaphor
of the hard black lump in my soul.

Crocus

How can such softness bear the strength
to throw off a winter's weight of snow?
Stubborn memory in stubborn root
heliotrope heliotrope
quick purple delirium
covering, pushing back
these too-close hills to mountains,
distant, perfect
as a child might draw them—
mountains you can count the flowers on.

Crayograph/Heintzman

I imagined each of the eight was linked
in some mysterious magical way
to keys I could play the piano in.
Red was loud C clownlips major.
Yellow was E, brilliant with sunsharps.
Blue the primal waters, before
the First Light of A,
low rumbling birth of sound
on Creation's first new day.
This made F green, and D an orange whim.
(I always coloured my elephants orange
because in dreams they spoke to me in D.)
Black B shone panthersleek, sharp-ribbed,
five sharps not easily tamed to the hand.
Purple Royal B flat trumpet fanfare.
Brown is the colour of silence—
earth-breath held in dormancy,
containing all sound.

My children used CRAYOLA,
its full spectrum ready-made—
sixty-four different shades of my eight
each with descriptive prescriptive name
from jungle green to tangerine
their only task to choose from what was there,
no need to meld imagination's hues.
Small wonder that my son at four was sad
because there was no "special" green
for the scaly beast he'd drawn and titled,
"Dragon looking forward to Christmas,"
or a black that was dull, not shiny
for the "witch who'd died of depressment."

Pieces of Eight

Pieces of eight, the bright parrot cried.
I'd colored the picture in the book—
the eight colours—broken bits of crayons
PRANG. My first experience of brand names.
PRANG! An onomatopoiea
of metal on cold metal. Daddy's old Colt
clanging against my crib bars.
PRANG. Conflation of two forbidden words
I'd heard my brothers use a lot.
Prang crayons. Worth the spanking I got
for breaking my brother's favorite red.
On purpose.

What potency there is in crayons.
A visual parrot, I couldn't draw
so I traced the parrot's outline
again and again—eight times in all,
and feathered each to my choosing
except the last I left all white
with only a crimson eye and throat.
I'd learned about primary colours—
blue for the sky and yellow for the sun
but red for blood that screams and pounds
behind the thin, thin walls of eyes forced shut—
screams like the parrot's strangulated voice,
not understood by its keepers
till they've taught it to say
what it cannot understand.

Nightmares

I
Sabre-toothed tiger acrouch
on the roof over the only door
of my burning house
waiting, knowing
the pads of his feet
could stand more heat
than my pale soles.
He could always
wait me out,
dismember,
eat me
up.

II
As
I am
chased
exhausted
over rough stubble
by a huge angry bull
slower and slower I run
until I am unable to move.
He's getting closer. I scream
but can not awaken myself
or the deaf, oblivious farmer
who ploughs an adjoining field.
Not all nightmares are ended
before the tiger pounces
before the bull's horn
finds your back,
before you hit
the ground
dead.

The Mole-Knight

Hideously faithful to his lady/victim
he stood in the shadow of the chimney
that warmed my attic room
His plumed helmet brushed the ceiling
his armour rasped the mortar
that oozed from between the bricks
His form would change when I entered sleep
to begin, in darkness, dread-slow descent
down the open stairs of nightmare's spidery cellar
The mole-knight would be there, waiting
compressed into a golden-copper ball
rolling madly about the rough concrete floor
As I'd reach the halfway point on the stairs
he would roll underneath the staircase
and metamorphose back
rise up six feet tall, black
from his round metallic egg
armed and armoured, his sword drawn
to slice between the stairtreads
and cut off my feet at the ankles
I'd look down, see the crimson ooze
then try, with icyclumsy fingers
to pick up my bloodslippery feet.
but when I bent, the sword returned
to sever my hands at the wristbones
The blood ran through the open stair
dark red in the darkness of the cellar
I'd always awaken as the next swing
sliced through my screaming throat

Nuisance Grounds

The poison-green combine, whose flaking paint
has survived its more solid metal parts,
hulks useless, monstrous on the skyline,
unable to settle into decent rot,
much less venerable entropy,
awkward in deserted limbo between
obsolescence and antiquity.

Our trash, unfit for a public landfill
gets hauled away to the pasture
where rust-red Herefords graze,
and sometimes maim themselves
on the snaggle-teeth of old hayrakes
that have rusted to jagged treachery.

I found an early mouldboard plough—
wooden handles worn smooth and grey,
its shares were dulled, encrusted
with the dried blood of the earth,
the horse that pulled it so long dead
not even the old man remembers its name.

Wrought iron bedsteads—so many here
archaeologists will suspect it
the midden of some ancient brothel.
Or perhaps surmise the truth:
inhabitants so lazy
they mostly wore out beds.
But five washing machines bear witness
to a clean establishment—of its kind.

I took away a brown glass gallon-jug
intact, it didn't seem to belong there,
a golden-amber pumpkin growing
on tangled frozen vines of rusting cable
whose only other fruits were half-crushed cans,
their only flowers discarded chrome hubcaps
tendrilled with loose wild bedsprings.

Medium
Brown
Jug

Medium
Brown
Jug
Found
long-drained of
its piquant malt vinegar,
wrapped in protective newspapers
brought to town to be cleaned, polished
and filled with shimmering silver lunaria.
Its outer surface polished quickly bright,
but its inner stain, much harder to reach
is stuck, hardened, may never come out.
I've got it soaking in my basement sink,
filled again, with much stronger vinegar.
How much more cleaning will be needed
before it comes into main-floor daylight,
sits in a south window, revels in the sun,
its amber charm revealed and revealing
goldening the whole room around it,
holding aloft its delicate treasures?

Meadowlark

After thirty earth-deafening years
her voice is still high, still tentative
like the meadowlark, tuned only
to sing in happy diatonics
even as the rough plough pillages its nest.
She remembers me clearly yet fondly—
says I sound just like my mother.
I take this as proof of something
as endearing as our kinship.
I ask if she remembers
washing, brushing, braiding my hair.
She remembers the time I broke my arm,
and asks if I still play the piano.
The piano followed her to our house.
Laughter she brought with her.
My sister taught me to sight-read,
but it was this one, smaller, graceful,
who showed me how to play by ear,
taught me to play by heart, from the heart.

We catch up on families, illnesses, deaths
and are both reluctant to hang up the phone.
It has taken us back to our pain-filled parting,
and I want to wash the wounds that bear my brand.
But the voice on the phone, this lark on the wire,
has sung her own healing. I am confounded,
made clumsy by her sweet denial
that there's anything to forgive.

Pilgrimages

Pilgrimage '88

The train glides on toward Canterbury
through the greening orchards of Kent
too fast for any sense of wending
no nuns, no priests, no lusty gat-toothed weavers
and none of the commuters in this car
looks hopeful enough to be a pilgrim.

Outside a group of schoolboys play—
absurd man-miniatures in ties and blazers
As the train approaches, the bravest one
some distant grandson of Nicholas and Alisoun
whips down his public-school grey trousers
moons the passing train, and gaily waves.

Notes From Underground

The Stations of the Cross

Perhaps it's the names of the stations.
In the morning, fresh and full of purpose
I shun the purblind beggar at Victoria
whose once-blond curls are matted to his head.
But on the way home from South Bank
I make sure there's always a loose pound
for the sax player at Waterloo.
Once, at Piccadilly, very brave,
I turned half-way up the escalator
and began conducting the French horn player.

Paradise Regained: First Visit to Kew

What would Milton have made of the Tube?
A potent silver serpent
that goes up and down in the earth.
On the platform I always have
sufficient sense to stand well back
knowing how free I am to fall.
Stepping onto the train I become Eve.
The frequent stops are always there,
reminding me I could get off.
The signs are more like angelic warnings—
nothing so neutral as "EXIT"
they all say "WAY OUT."
Some even point to alternative
above-ground routes.
I stay on the train, taking
a certain pleasure from its motion
sinuous and legato as a snake
whose movements always start unsignalled—
the way it always is with a good seduction.

Gunnersby Station

The train is above ground here—almost—
if you don't count the concrete parkade walls
which constitute a gallery of dissent.
Here, just above the line where the urine
has killed off the rankest brambleberries,
the frustrated children of the new empire
have spent their pale chalksticks
and a small portion of their rage.
Their colourful Anglo-Saxon smut
will soon be covered by newer, blacker stuff.
Just outside the station a billboard
Mrs. Thatcher, lacquered, dentured, suited, pearled,
smiles in triumph over the caption,
"A woman's work is never done."
Obscenity is in the eye of the beholder.

Finding Uttoxeter

Johnson's Kiosk, Uttoxeter Market Square

Laborare est orare: to work is to pray

I first heard about it from my mother
when I was a high school student
reading Johnson and Boswell, wondering
if Johnson spoke so well because he saw
that Boswell copied every word, or if
Boswell wrote because of what he heard?
She told me of the simple monument—
Johnson had refused his father's request
to take books to Uttoxeter market.
Later, reviling himself, he walked
the forty miles from Lichfield,
stood bareheaded
in the rain for one whole day.
This permanent stone confession
of a failure of filial piety
stands—too big, too powerful
ever to be ignored. It's now
a magazine kiosk. Useful, prayerful.
Johnson would have approved.

"That Great Cham of Literature"

Born forty miles from his birthplace,
she never valued him.
Called him "that great sham of literature,"
Smollett would have smiled at her malapropism.
She refused to visit Lichfield,
not even to see the cathedral.
I used to tease her, accusing her
of being more stubborn than Johnson
but lacking his piety.
Perhaps she'd have relented
had she seen the small devil's head
carved in stone at the base of an arch,
laughing at the peasant skulls around him.
She'd have been delighted to see
the devil built right into the church,
not just slipping in through the choir loft.

Tobias Smollett referred to Johnson as "That Great Cham of Literature,"
meaning Khan (as in Genghis) or ruler.

St. Michael's, Stramshall

I can still recognize the Y in the road—
just like the photo taken 1912.
The church still watches over its dead
though the lorry traffic threatens their peace.
The only Black man in the parish
moves among the headstones with a scythe.
He looks askance at us foreigners
who would enter this place on a weekday.
I explain this was my mother's church.
He is too young to remember the name
but he knows the legend of the ancient yew
that stands sentry at the door. The cutting
brought from the holy land. I wonder if
my mother heard the story, and why
she never passed it on to me?
So much more than the bones of the dead
lies buried all around us.

Inside, the church is dark,
but I forgo the electric light,
new since she read her prayers
by windowlight from Gothic frames
each holding a black-limned pastel angel
standing on ribbons of printed words—
words she did pass on: "Faith, Hope, Charity,
and the greatest of these is love."
I'd remembered, because it stood alone
the only lesson she could believe in,
remember enough to teach her children
when every kind of famine and darkness
wrapped itself around her throat
and sat gorging on her chest.

Springtime in the Bull Pasture

Learn to enjoy the little things, she'd say,
when I wanted every dress in the wishbook.
I would sit on her warm but bony lap,
fingers pointing at each bright page.
We'd hear the dog bark, the truck pull up,
the crunch of tires on snow.
Then I'd feel through her thin cotton dress
a tensing of muscle, a hardening of—bone?
We'd both rise quickly, knowing.

He will be hungry, she'd say,
and go to pare potatoes, fry red meat.
The door would burst open, and in he'd charge,
snorting, steaming, cursing the cold.
The china cups she'd brought from England—
intact, but glazes long since crazed with age—
rattled in their apple-box cupboard
when his giant boots stomped off their snow.
I'd put away the catalogue and
set the table with dishes out of soap boxes.

One birthday lately, I took her a chain:
Twenty-four carat gold, wrapped in silk
in a lapis lazuli marmalade jar.
The man who made the chain asked, "Why
twenty-four? Eighteen would do as well.
Twenty-four carat clasps don't hold."
Twenty-four carat gold, I said.
He shrugged and said, "It won't last."
But I have seen one small wood violet
that has blossomed each Spring for sixty years
in the bull pasture.

Mediation

He never forbade her reading, unless
you consider him carefully timing
his rare attempts at conversation
to coincide with her attempts to read.
So she weaned herself of even the desire,
claiming Chaucer had a filthy mind,
and Shakespeare wasn't much better.
So I asked her opinion of Dickens:
"Oh, yes. Such a moral man."
I could never tell her about Ellen Ternan.
She proof-read my thesis on the Troilus,
seizing upon each typo as if
perfection in my text would overcome
both Pandarus and Chaucer, maybe even
save Criseyde from sudden Diomede.
She knew about willing the body to
the man who'd taken possession of it.

My Mother's House

True pilgrims, shrine to shrine, we go on foot
from Johnson's kiosk in the market square
past half-timbered shops new in 1510
past the yellow brick constabulary
across a stream she'd call a brook
and up the hill to Old Stoneyford Terrace
new in 1900. She was born there, 1907.
The first in the row is burned out, abandoned.
At our approach, a pair of mourning doves
flies out of a paneless, blackened window
their wingbeats like her rapid troubled breath
in flight from her pain-wracked blackened body——
body so thin it seemed a smoked glass case
that covered but could not conceal her wounds.
I cry out not so much surprised as pained
at the reading of this message
that beats at the heart with wings
frail as her final resistance to death.
The last sight of her is revivified—
her great waves of white hair
her olive skin braised to aubergine
her last miraculous whispered words
"It's a beautiful, beautiful life."

8 Stoneyford Terrace, Uttoxeter

Number 8, at the end, is newly restored
doors and new-framed windows Lincoln green,
defiant of Staffordshire reds and blues
but with the traditional convex panes
stuck in at random among the rest.
Would this account for her strange "blind spots?"
her peculiar ways of seeing things?
A black-and-white cat yawns from a flowerpot
where he warms the soil for planting.
From inside the house an infant cries.
Breathless, I ring the bell.

A smiling young woman opens the door.
I stammer out the purpose of our visit.
She welcomes us into her kitchen,
explaining that they've not lived there long.
The renovations are not complete.
She runs a hand down scrubbed pine cupboards,
"We've kept the original wood throughout."
I can almost hear my mother—or
is it my grandmother saying, "Waste not, want not."
Their daughter, she tells us, is three weeks old.
Later, I realize her birth coincides
with a death a world away.
I want to tell this younger granny of mine,
"Call her Eleanor this time. She'd like that."

First Love

Names she remembered were few
but constant over the years,
so I had to ask about Jack Griffin.
My cousin drove me to his house,
the neatest cottage in Broomy Close.
He collected porcelain horses—
He patted one, saying, "I imagine
that Nell became a great horsewoman.
She was such a fine dancer. So graceful."
With his wife listening, forbearing,
he remembered it all, from the first grade
hand-holding through the dancing lessons
to their initials carved in the ash tree.
He showed us a school picture, every name
and face a story, and the question,
"Did she mention any other names?"
How pleased he was to know
that he and the vicar's daughters—
the ones who gave dancing lessons—
were the only inhabitants
of the village in her mind.

April in the Peloponnese

Beulah poses patiently, for the second time
in as many days. Yesterday she wept,
overcome with joy in my children,
long-lost kin from the New World.
Today she smiles when we explain
how yesterday's film was destroyed.
(Her neighbour's goat looks over the fence
as if it knows it's being talked about.)
Beulah doesn't laugh, but I know she wants
to throw back her head, remember Dionysos,
sing the song of the goat, and cackle.
But she is bound by her tight grey scarf,
grey with black oblong shapes, miniature coffins.
Beulah prepares for widowhood, or death
bending toward the ground,
seeing only the black soil outside her house.
She ignores the great gardenia bush
that threatens to force its roots
through the straining wooden tub.
The plant has more buds than Beulah has years
but Beulah is too short, too stooped to see them.
A few at the top have begun to open.
I bend toward a creamy centre, eager
to be again seduced by that scent,
fill my lungs with a thousand memories.
But the wind has suddenly shifted,
sifting the glorious with the goat.
I recall the gardenias of a forgotten courtship,
a December wedding, a December funeral.
The goat bleats, wanting feeding, or milking.

Hellenic Bells

I

I bought the first Greek bells I ever heard
here, on this arid frontier.
Seduced by their sound,
their Byzantine abundance—seven
strung random on an opulent orange cord.
I had in mind no purpose with their purchase,
no goat, no cows to tie them on
no need for me to wear them
to scare away wild beasts on mountain hikes.
They were rusted, as if long-submerged
and their sound still told of water,
they smelled of ancient bronze
and sang of Hesiod's happy flocks
of days before time and Muses round the spring.

II

It's Holy Week in Thessaloniki.
Cats are asleep on red tiled roofs
ignoring the turtles who copulate
with slow, noisy effort.
High up in the Old Town we walk
showing our barbarism by being out
when natives sleep, or make slow love
inside their tall cool houses.
We seek shelter from the sun in a church.
The dark inside is not dispelled by the candles
nor by their reflections on all the gold.
The little black-clad women
absorb the light,
only to distill it into their eyes
and send it searing home
like Clytaemnestra's knife.

III

The city wakes up sluggish.
It's unseasonably hot for Easter.
Windows are opened, yawned out of.
The turtles have resettled themselves
in opposite corners of the garden
to continue their own siestas.

IV

Our hostess seats us in her garden.
The scene is like a travelogue set
or a record jacket for old *kantades*.
The house is tall white, stuccoed,
with tall thin windows that look
like icons' eyes, dark-rimmed and sombre.
The jasmine stirs into scented life
mixing with, then conquering the roses.
The Macedonian wine is cool. We're thirsty.
A dark-eyed girl appears on a balcony,
an icon of this happy time and place.
Laughing down to us, she seems
poised between childhood's days of roses
and jasmine-scented nights of womanhood.

V

Thessaloniki is full of churches—
a city of Byzantine domes and bells.
This evening they begin early,
muffled by the thick, exhausted air
then louder, rising over the smog band
to call the faithful, and the atheists too.
Church here is not only for believers.
The sun sets quickly behind Olympus.
We walk down the hill in a golden ringing dusk
into the church that was so dim
this sun-stroked afternoon.
Now a thousand candles light the gilded dome,
the gold-robed bishop's golden crosier gleams.

But even here, the smaller bells that swing
from the sweat-stained hands of altar boys
to punctuate the chanted liturgy
are muffled by candlesmoke,
incense, and the crowd.

VI

We drive into Dion's pristine morning
before the roaring season
of diesel tourist buses
but after the archaeologists
have left their dig, defeated....
We walk the site, and mark the line
where their money ran out.
This was Apollo's sacred city
laid out in perfect order.
The silence here is perfect too,
and then we hear a tingling shimmer of song.
The herd approaches, the bells appear
shining, polished by the silken brisket
clear, well-tuned with daily use.
Each bell sounds small, but each is heard.
Is this where the ancients learned democracy?
The goatherd leads his flock across Apollo's ruined home
Oblivious of us, ignorant of the god
but he knows each animal by name.
He wears gumboots, and a long woollen cloak.
His shepherd's crook goes back to Hesiod.
Like the bells, its usefulness is clear.
I remember my Greek bells at home,
where they hang on the back door.
When I go home, I must move them to the front.

LOUISIANA POEMS

Enlightenment Conference, March 1993

All day on planes, incommunicado,
smelling of tension and plane plastic,
trying not to remember
what a stewardess once told me
about occupational hazards of her job—
the only moisture in the air on planes
is from people's armpits.

Arriving, deplaning,
the air was strangely familiar—
not warm and moist like the Gulf Coast armpit I know.
"Feels like snow," my friend said.
We both laughed, then buttoned our coats
against the rising storm.
It's still a hard place to get into—
ask the Cajuns. They'll tell you
there's no easy access to heaven.
We were later to discover, as plane
after promised plane was late from Atlanta,
it was harder to leave than hell.

Nothing was as expected—
the airport taxi was old and rusted,
The sign on the door read *Fini Cabs*.
I hoped it wasn't in Italian.
The driver held a home-made cellular phone
in his only hand. Judy, ever logical,
turned to me and whispered,
"What do you suppose he's steering with?"
I asked why she thought the car was being steered.

The driver was southern-friendly.
Asked us where we'd come from.
Despite the southwest gale that was blowing
he asked us if we'd brought the cold down from Canada.
Every direction must seem like up from here.
He told us he was from Persia, but was
proud to be an American citizen.
I wondered how the State Genealogist
would deal with his particular shade.

Crown Sterling Suite

The lobby boasts a seven-storey atrium,
gardens, and a pond that's home
to two pair of courting ducks
whose discretion is admirable
considering the season.

In the lobby we sit down to wait
for the one-armed taxi driver—
by now we know his story
of pain and persecution "back home."
He claims to be happy here—a wife,
two black-haired, sloe-eyed children
who ride with him and his fares.
(Once he even brought his wife,
but I think that was just to meet us.
We were sure that a few more days
would acquaint us with the mother-in-law.)

This morning calm is broken
by a yelling Aryan horde—a team
of fat blond boys in white track suits
with REDEMPTORIST WOLVES and wolf-heads
emblazoned on their chests.
In my part of the world children's shirts
bear slogans like "SAVE THE WOLVES."
As they race among the sofas
making mayhem among the cushions,
laying waste the floral arrangements
that grace the ebony Broadwood.
I fear for this fine old piano
they are trying to force open
but fail to stop their assault.
Who will save this last refrain
of antebellum song
from this all-devouring pack
of *sois-disant* redeemers?

Harmony, Grits

The Cajuns remember Evangeline
but no one remembers which Louis
gave his name to this swampy place
more aptly named Langoustiana
Duke here means David, not d'Orleans.
Cajuns stare openly at us, strangers
tumbling, shivering, off the charter bus.
Inside the place called Betty's on the Bayou,
The buffet line meanders fat-, salt-heavy
like the silt-laden river outside—
tending to stall in bayous of stale talk.
In the room the scholars come and go,
talking no deconstruction or po-mo.
(Tonight it's Reconstruction and fais do-do.)
There is time to gaze at everything—
I examine the ceiling where Spanish moss
hangs greybeard-ghostly from the rafters—
bayou fog made solid from greasy boudin steams,
the walls are hung with stretched hides
and leg-hold traps not rusty enough.
At the end of the line is an empty pirogue—
Charon has just slipped next-door for a beer.
By the bandstand a stuffed ocelot
arches his dusty back in posthumous protest
against the nails that pierce his paws in Cajun crucifixion,
his glass eyes dimmed by the dust kicked up by countless feet
not much freer than his own eternal twostep.

Espresso Bar in the Cortana Mall

The couple behind us are arguing
over how they live their lives—
TV or not TV, that is their question.
My friend, whose sensibilities
are more finely tuned than mine,
flees in search of something sweet.
It is now my turn to be served.
I order, but the girl's attention
is claimed by a louder voice.
When she turns back to me she says,
"Did you axe me for an expresso?"
"Mocha latte, please." But when I see her
reach beneath the counter and haul out
an industrial-sized can of Nestle's Quik,
I cancel the order and walk away.
Perhaps it's a semiotic problem.
Signs here, as the locals say, just don't signify.
The *fleurs-des-lis* here all have four parts,
and I suspect the Cajun triangle
also has four sides.

Dancin' at the Fais Do-Do

I've never come south without you before.
I want to see it all for you as well,
remember, wrap it, bring it home.
This 18th-century conference is laid on thickly—
accents, sessions, bonhommie and boudin.
The bus hauls freezing scholars—
no southerners were prepared for this—
to a snowy swamp outside of town
for tourist purposes a bayou.
A dance-hall-cum-bar-cum-restaurant
sprawls on stilts at the slow dark water's edge,
a balcony for tourists also serves
as roof over the alligators' heads
"tourist trap" indeed.
But who's to say we've not been warned
by the leg-hold traps, the empty pirogues
and the row of gators' heads that sits
wide-smiling at the dancers?
Who will buy this death that grins ?

Outside on the veranda, I'm engulfed
by cold mist rising from still-warm water,
an illustration for *The Inferno*,
and remember that we did not use the bus,
but rode out in *Fini Cabs*, not *Mezzo*.
Here is where self comes to self, alone
in the penumbra of the cloud
between the leering dancehall lights
and the menacing fog
that rises noiselessly.

Back inside, the oldest emeritus,
black-suited, black-tied but not quite black-tie
dances with the dogged foot of one
who knows all the steps but has stopped
taking the next one for granted.
His stiff white hair dishevelled now,
his age-polished cheeks aglow,
he seeks younger and younger partners,
in panting defiance of
the fog advancing toward him
in the grey uniform
of the confederacy of death.

He asks me to dance—I know that tune!
It's one you and I both heard as children—
three thousand miles apart.
"Rose of San Antone"—the singer stumbles,
can't remember the words. I could help out
but don't. Enlightenment manners have me
dancing with a strange old man—
"Lips so sweet and tender,
like petals fallen apart,"
and I think of you, locked in a stone castle
high above a swift cold river,
unkissed, unkissing,
with a music critic and no music,
with a dancer, and no dance.
Self, when I see you again,
we will know one another new,
your song, my dance.

Tempean Echoes

Hospital Passing

Every morning we pass the hospital
where their father worked
where they both were born.
It's being demolished, slowly.
One day, as we drove past the site
we saw the wrecking ball take aim,
then make its drunken swing
through his old office window.
I think we all expected to hear
his ghost give a good Greek curse,
see the leaden ball stopped short
by his stout lead-apron shield.

Across the parking lot
the old maternity wing is gone,
but I've managed to salvage three bricks—
one for each child and one for me.
Only blackened steel pillars remain,
rising tall, erect, from the rubble,
like a burned-out forest,
reminders of a fierce, brilliant flame.

For Zoé

This afternoon you watched
as they buried your grandfather
You've always seen things
more clearly than most
Tonight, on my patio
you saw for the first time
Aurora Borealis
They reminded me of you
they danced with such grace
Bodies invisible
in tutus of pastel light
You said they reminded you
of chalkboards just erased
of coloured chalk
But I know you had read
in the language of heaven
Dounya's message of love
soundless, self-effacing.

Geologic Time

for Paul

The geomorphology lab TA
brash Californian youth abrading
my widow's adamantine grief
dissolving the cinder-cone from the heart
with nothing more than his own fragile joy—
shared with my son. He taught
the morphology of so much more
than the earth we cavilled over.

Eons later, my son tends his two boys.
I've remarried, and met his wife.
He's not so brash any more—he's learned
the rhythms of the earth, from the tidal power
that flows in her soft Nova Scotian voice.

I'll never ask him now
the indelicate question
of what he saw
when he looked at me,
an igneous mass, hardness ten?
or a geode waiting for the fracture?

Vasiliko

I
In Greece young village girls
are given pots of basil
to set on their windowsills
to tend with hope and care.
The village boys are taught
to assess all wifely talents
by the luxuriance of this bush.

II
The pot I set out on the patio
produced almost no leaves,
blossoms that attracted wasps,
then went directly to seed.
I've dug it up and brought it in
It looks like bonsai—
forced into age and wisdom
before its time.

III
My son's name is Vasilis,
after his father's father,
his grandfather's grandfather,
and back into Linear B.
I tell him he is a linear V.

Chinese Lanterns

I

Dried Chinese Lanterns
trembling on their stiff branches
a heart-hollow sound

green-veined orange globes
tumescent paper-thin pods
anxious to dash themselves
against the hard dry ground
they've sprung from—
suicidal spilling
of bright red seed

II

I ride in the back seat holding the flowers
dried Chinese Lanterns for my new office
Their whispered rustlings make me think
of the slave who rode behind Caesar
on his chariot, ringing a small bell
audible only to Caesar
to remind a god
of mortality

My son rides
in the front now
his six-foot frame is too big for
the back. As he studies every move
his dad makes driving, I'm wondering
how I can plant a whispered warning,
Go carefully. We are all mortal.

Brahms Duo

I

Hearing the German Requiem again
after all the storms are past
I remember now that other time
sitting in a concert hall
feeling if I could only
hold my breath long enough
I would diminish with a phrase
and be borne across the bright city
on a dark blue tide of music
and alight on your windowsill,
a perfect close-position cadence
quivering, but intact

II

I played a Brahms intermezzo
not to entertain you
but to provide an interlude
while you went to use the phone
I didn't plan the performance
The sun light came in
with the bright golden E major chords
that thickened, warmed, then broke
into delicate sonic rills
beneath my newly articulate fingers
The last note held,
intact, but quivering

A Tempean Echo

It was the perfect lunch. Your face,
your hair still golden from the sun
framed by Olympus rising behind your shoulders
praised by an eagle that appeared above you
I felt like Semele in her secret glade
You marvelled at the Aegean blue
the clear Tempean sky
I marvelled at your eyes—
a truer blue, and clearer
We drank the cool Macedonian wine
I don't remember what we ate that day
but I remember the circular plain below
where the muses danced to Apollo's lyre
Like us, protected by the joy of their dance
from the slavering envious beasts
who eye our sunlit circle
from their dark and loveless forest.

Aloe (Quaecumquae) Vera

In an elevated glass walkway,
a small oasis of transition
between a noisy mall and the library
sits a tenure of aloe.
Almost perfect plants—
softest, silvery celadon green
hard, thick-to-pointed spikes
that spread in all directions
like arms that wave in muted exhortation.
Medicinal, their juice will heal a cut.
But from years of walking that glassed-in trail,
from years of seeing the same small heart
cut white in the green
enclosing two sets of initials
and pierced by an arrow, I've learned
that even on the plant that heals men's wounds
the scars of love are permanent.

Educating Hester

Sitting at the side of the classroom
alone, self-marginalized, a little
older than the other freshmen
but she'd camouflaged her body
in jeans, sweaters, boots.
Her attention never wavered
even though I sometimes glimpsed
pain creasing her forehead.
For the first two months of term,
when I directed a question her way
she flinched, moved her hands about
in mute anguish that surprised me
but one tries not to speculate
on their private problems

She was quiet through Jane Austen
nor could the Romantic poets unlock
her voice. Shaw's willful Cleopatra
she seemed to take to better.

Then we read *The Scarlet Letter*
and she brought me her essay
thirty-five heart-wrung hard-lived pages
in a red folder decorated with
a black silhouette of her own profile,
wonderful hair billowing over
a red lace "A" with gold dust
glued underneath.
It scatters itself over my desk
into every other folder
over the insipid naivete
over the smug judgements
of the fundamentalist virgin
and the carefree class floozy alike
I can only hope it will cling—
bits of an emblem of her
golden, generous lesson.

Cupid of Port Arthur

Mouth open, brushing my teeth
no need to consult the mirror
I turn to my favourite photo
a late-40's black-and-white
your parents walking
you between them
street-photographer's dream and they knew it
your father holds your upstretched hand
acknowledging with naive pride
his own good looks, and yours
and his genial lust for your mother
No signs of the death that would claim him
before he could share a father's pride
with you

Your mother has let the symmetry down
she doesn't hold your other hand
and her smile is for the camera
acknowledging adoration
no sign of future torments
betrayed by her heavy-lashed eyes

Your broad forehead bears an infant frown
your mouth is open in a perfect "O"
You are looking off to your right
at something outside the picture frame
as you do now—speaking to someone else
looking at me. I imagine you
looking far to the northwest
to the picture of me
framed in enamel

I rinse, then turn to see you here, now
both parents' features, your own smile
giving back my adoration
your mouth still the honey'd "O"
perfect, for me

Kalispera, Aphrodite Calling

There were three warning calls first
two hours before. But her herald was silent
not even breathing on the other end
then, at eight o'clock of a January evening
Aphrodite herself. No last name.
She addresses me only in demotic Greek
as if I've known her all my life
I'm unprepared to speak
my tongue is lost to those sounds
and if it weren't, the tangled strands
of love, loss, death, desertion balk
each other like playgoers thronging
from a burning theatre.

The urgency of the voice,
its rapid high soprano
that verges on the shrill,
confuses me further.
Aphrodite should speak sweet and low
and never mention Macedonia.

Hours after her call I realize
I have been favoured—
called person-to-person
by the goddess of love
and though I'm not sure what she said
I shall climb the stairs tonight
with even more anticipation
than usual

Deja Vu

Coming into this room, something
in the air, not just the luxury
of lilacs crowding the stage—
scent, irresistible awakener
of memories from other lives—
yes, this was a ballroom
and now the ear again is pierced
to the heart by remembered sounds
untuned piano's watery staccato
violins' unsynchronous vibrato
the waltz from *Faust* that blossoms me
into a flowery whirl of violet silks
full-length dove-grey gloves of kid
with even more tiny hook buttons
than the tall dove-grey kid boots

I resist, eyes firmly closed
ears receiving only the wavelengths
of a past I don't remember
my nose still trying on
the delicate shape of my grandmother's
to reclaim the essence of an earlier evening

I am clapped awake, wide-eyed,
the lavender silk rustles off
the stage of mind
somewhere a hundred tiny buttons
will be unhooked, slowly,
with a tiny silver instrument

Leather Weddings

Lunchroom Lioness

"You can lead a whore to culture
but you can't make her think."
Dorothy Parker

Four inches of heel plus three more of mane
make her almost as tall as me.
Her pride gives further elevation—
enough that she needn't see me.
She has not offered me a look
at the lingerie catalogues
she passes around at coffee breaks
but I can tell from the comments
that this is a new kind of tup'er wear,
and nothing practical is being sold—
but perhaps practicality, like beauty,
is an individual thing. Who knows
how many hours have been saved
by her crotchless panties, her cut-out bras?

I've seen pictures she took of a wedding—
her brother, well-oiled, mustachioed, tattooed,
in a black leather tuxedo, with boots
his bride in traditional white—
leather and lace, leather and lace
repeated twice so we'd understand
leather garterbelt, leather bra,
lace bustier, lace petticoat and stockings
then leather gown, leather Stetson, lace veil,
white suede boots with detachable fringes
(in case it got muddy)

73

A four-passenger helicopter
was chartered to transport guests
to the wedding, held on the highest hill
outside of Norman Wells at one a.m.
midsummer's night. I did not dream this.
Who could dream a cigarette held so tight
between the bride's lips that lines formed
like pleats from her nose to her mouth
to match the giant pleats
on the shoulders of the leather gown?
Who could dream the extravagance
of fingernails so long she could neither do
nor undo the buttons on her dress?

The picture I like the most
was the candid shot of the bride
hitching up her skirts with one hand
and attacking an unknown guest
with a whisky bottle clutched in the other.
Leola said it wasn't cheap rye neither.
And that bottle was a virgin.

Aubade

We always read the morning papers
together, in our bed of white linens,
sharing orange juice, coffee, news.
It's such a ritual I never smell
an orange, coffee, or newsprint
without sniffing for your scent,
mixed with my perfume.

You sometimes read the personals aloud—
rented lines cast from their own
inner darks into a blacker out-there—
the only pain you ever cause me—
that helpless pity for the lonely

But this morning not even pity is roused—
"Large white man wants woman."
A serendipitous shake of the paper
presents these solutions for his problem:

JOVAN WHITE MUSK FOR MEN
All the power.
But not overpowering.
A clean, long-lasting
scent that lets you be you.
So you can have her.
Subtle. But always clear
about who you are.
Easygoing. Without
compromising what you
want or what you're
going to get.
Unmistakably male.

Or, for the less aggressive, perhaps
JOVAN SEX APPEAL COLOGNE SPRAY FOR MEN
Now you don't have to
be born with it.
This provocative stimulating
blend of rare spices and herbs
was created by man for
the sole purpose of attracting
women. At will.
Man can never have too much.

On the same page, for young undertakers
or necrophiliacs of any age
there is GRAVITY.

I almost believe you when you say
you're going to market a new cologne
aimed at the Large White Man,
and call it
GET LUCKY.

Apples

I

Peeling this mythical fruit for a pie,
I ponder Paris and his bad judgment
but they never learn, do they?
They still reward the whores
and ignore the good girls.
What was wrong with Athena?
A good strong woman
who could throw a pot,
cultivate the olive grove and
probably butter her share of phyllo.
She'd have known what to do with that apple.
But I suspect it was Venus's soft-cupped hand
around the full firm fruit reminding him
how her breasts would feel—

II

Pome fruit that Milton made into poem fruit—
Doubtless it would have pleased him a lot
to know that the seeds are cyanotic,
he'd have taken it as proof
of Eve's evil at the core.

My Milton professor hated Milton,
claimed *Paradise Lost* a failure because
"Perfection is boring. There is only
one way to be good, but a thousand
interesting ways to be bad."
As I graze the produce aisles
picking up each variety of apple,
smelling it, I think of the professor
and want to take him a basket of apples
saying, no, there are a thousand ways
to enjoy the good. But he has me fixed
in another story about women and apples.

My favourite story is his own.
When he played tuba in his high school band
his schoolmates threw apples into the bell.
He's still sputtering them out.

III

Milton rhymed at the age of eight
Newton, slower, was twenty-three
before he invented calculus
to measure the orbit of the moon.
One year later, *Paradise Lost*
justified the ways of God to man.
The next year Newton responded
with the reflecting telescope:
the heavens were indeed telling—
this time speaking for themselves.
Newton's mythical apple falling
through Milton's crystal spheres, made
a plumbline for a greater Chain of Being

IV

There's winningness about the apple—
The Big Apple
Apple Records
Apple Computers
Apple of the eye.
A most useful symbol—
When my feminist step-daughter
decided to marry her live-in of five years,
they sent out desktop-printed announcements
with borders of the computer's logo,
the apple already bitten into.

Club Sandwiches

Faculty Club, Saturday Afternoon

I don't trust the double glazing of the wall of window in the bar this frozen afternoon. Waiting my turn to read poems, I order a hot buttered rum, on the principle of warming from the inside. I hold it closely, sipping slowly. I watch the paper birches in the courtyard, their bark wind-whipped into hoary tatters. Two frail emeriti near the glass wall sit holding time like the grail in their hands, sipping it (mixed with pale lager) slowly, as if to draw it out upon the tongue without disturbing it. I catch bits of their conversation: "February is still suicide month." "Yes. The bottom of the icy slope of January. The valley of the the shadow of debt." "From Christmas past." I hesitate to read. The birch trees are already growing new bark. But men....

Faculty Club, Saturday Evening

Upstairs now, in the formal dining room. This is the night of the week ties are required. We are greeted by the waiter. He's an Alberta boy but tonight he is Kreshta, affecting a limp and Hungarian accent. (Sometimes he's Jeeves, replete with silver salver, napkin adrape over one arm, the other arm behind him.) He drinks club vodka by the tumbler. It looks like water so he drinks it like water. But he never stumbles or slurs his words. Across the room, in their usual corner, the husband-and-wife psychiatrists are having their regularly scheduled fight. When the pasta arrives, as if on cue, or perhaps from some subliminal suggestion from Kreshta, they ceremoniously exchange dishes of *linguine alle vongole* and *tagliatelle à salmone*—over each other's heads. But they never raise their voices. It will be dessert and coffee before the ancient countess in the other corner bares her breasts and declaims to the whole room that "it was these breasts, these beautiful breasts, that saved me in the Revolution."

Music Lessons

Madame Maurier didn't want to teach me—
said I was too young. I had to prove
I was literate, housebroken, and that
the bottle of Airwick on the piano
would not be needed while she taught me.
She combed my hair while I played my scales
and sang along in a smoky contralto
to my sonatinas.

My second teacher, a wizened nun
carried her own strange antiseptic smell,
would grasp my hands in her own
cold barren talons, and wheeze
"You know the Parable of the Talents."
I never could bring myself to ask
why God would squander his talents
on a heathen like me.

My city teacher was Swiss-French,
smelled of wine and pipe tobacco.
One day his son's pet boa constrictor
crawled into the fur collar of my coat—
seeking any heat in that frigid house.
As it moved from the collar and down my arm,
he used it to demonstrate legato motion:
"the beginning must be imperceptible."

And one day, when I'd played quite badly,
he grabbed my hips and squeezed, staccato,
"The music must come from—HERE!"
I didn't go back, despite evidence
of his eagerness to teach me.

Wordpower

I
In the physiotherapist's waitingroom
my own book forgotten at home
I pick up a Reader's Digest.
Doesn't everyone?
"It pays to enrich your Word Power."
I've yet to find a new word there
and I try to remember not to use
whatever I see on that page.
Would you trust a company
that got rich leaving out words?

II
The walk home from physio
is on fresh concrete sidewalks.
Every hundred meters or so
there are words at my feet:
PRIM POWER and an arrow
spraypainted in a fleshy pink.
I know it is some cryptic sign
from one hard hat to another,
but I can't erase a mental picture
of white-gloved grannies gathering
in some antimacassared parlour
to plot a Restoration
of mannerly morality.

Minnesota Fatuous

He's traded his cue for a talking stick,
advertised his balls for sale, and now
this red-faced, beefy iron man
is spreading tallow-skeins of outworn myth
over bones of primitive butchery
and wrapping up the lot
in shaggy lust-warbled hides
setting others of his kind
on fire with half-burnt offerings—
flames to light the forgotten path
back to the cave.

A Short Course in Modern Poetry

William Butler Yeats
gyrates.

Ezra Pound?
Of mind unsound.

Hopkins our Father?
Off-rhymes and sprung blather.

Hardy?
No bard'e.

Auden?
An odd'n.
Oh yes, my dear.
Wynstan is queer.

Stephen Spender?
Sincere and tender,
loved to prate
about the great.

Dylan Thomas?
A latter-day Comus.

Thomas Stearns he
really burns me.
Greek quotes
and footnotes.
T.S. the Great?
Impotentate.

Sexton?
No text on.
The girdle's
the hurdle.

Ted Hughes
needs no muse.
Blow
that Crow.

Who is Sylvia?

September Songs

I

Past Summer's noon in our garden
the bees ignore the bright but scentless flowers
suck only at the fragrant basil blossoms
The largest of the hive—I call him Caesar—
goes to it with such zest he falls to earth
The white bloom covers him like a shroud
He lies on his back, a fallen hero
besotted by perfume

II

This Sunday morning I've come out early
to check the garden trapline
I count the swollen pinkish bodies
stretched out in saucers of beer
They must have come to last night's party
as eagerly as slugs can come
in their slow hermaphroditic way
I know just how Lucrezia Borgia felt
surveying her banquet hall
on a Sunday morning

Pruning

Flirting, he asked her to edit his work.
I'm a gardener, she said, not a poet.
He persisted. She acquiesced—took
pruning knife to apical adjectives,
scraped away a few rough spots,
secateured a not-quite-sentient sentence,
used loppers—that was fun—for one dead stanza.
A poem needs shape like a shrub.
If she hadn't picked up her chain saw
he might have stayed for the Roundup.

Mammiotics

A mammogram has been ordered
and I am sent to the Breast Centre.
The reception aureola rug is dotted
with puffy chintz-covered nipplepink chairs.
In the inner room the red-brown carpet
has spread like a period ran amok.
Exposed here, in this female place
the kindly staff call everyone "Dear,"
and try for a lot of eye contact.

Panic here is collective,
palpable as a lumpy breast
pendulous over hands clasped
in their own gnarled terror.

The patients do not meet each other's eyes.
Is it the shame of knowing
that woman's primary signifier,
the site of sexual semiotics,
is site of the primary sign
of the indication to remove
the signifier itself, and with it
love claimed by the signifier
but not necessarily by the signified?

I contemplate the sign on the desk:
MAMMOGRAPHY
Mammalia—class
Mammary glands—zoology class
Mamma—infant's first word
Ma'am—southern respect
for a lady, with the sound
of femininity in it.

I recall a medical library job
The CIBA breast atlas the most-used book.
I learned from that not to date med students.

I am called, by first name only—
insult binding onto me the indignity
of the hospital-green-paper blouse—
I am led into the half-dark room
and told, "You might feel some pressure."
I am measured, pummelled, and queried,
"What size cup do you usually wear?"
I look at the vast tray in front of me
that looks like a butcher's scale
and murmur in confusion, "demitasse."

My flesh is pulled, flattened,
and pressed in a lucite vise.

Leaving, I seriously doubt if
I'll ever eat Chicken Kiev again.

Mind/Body Blues

Exploring the mind/body problem
I wander between the late sixteenth
and early twentieth centuries
searching the Enlightenment for the mean
between Descartes and Skinner
straddling the barbed-wire fence
that keeps dualist and behaviorist apart.
I should be glad, for once, to miss the point.

The eighteenth-century medicine men
stress the power of body over mind
As my body declines
to do what the mind requires of it
the problem is consumed
by metaphors from my abandoned kitchen
A lemon meringue tart becomes Descartes
A hunk of raw meat for dinner is Skinner.

The anatomist of melancholy
from the seventeenth century
tells me it's my mind
exporting its misery
to the body's extremities.
My twentieth-century physician
takes my history, then tells me briskly
I'm exhausted. And clinically depressed.
I'd prefer the term 'scholar's melancholy.'

I contemplate my recalcitrant hands.
The diamond on my finger,
like the love that placed it there,
produces its own bright fire
its full spectrum of light refracted
reminds me that my own range
of refractoriness has been diminished.
I don't see red so easily these days
and these blues aren't in G sharp minor
but one analogy at last is clear:
brain is to zircon
as diamond is to mind.

Insomnia

*pahoehoe.— (pa-hoi-hoi)"pillow lava," a Hawaiian term for basaltic lava
flows typified by smooth, billowy, or ropy surface.*

Tossed up from nightmare's volcano,
consciousness hardening instantly
pillows now comfortless as pahoehoe.
The body prison turns on
all its inside lights.
Torture's tradition is of the night:
head throbs fuchsia neon
joints incandesce with pain
muscles, marrow, molten
eyes burn lava-red
too hot to close.

Rise silently, do not disturb
the kinder half of the marriage bed.
Don't look back at that face
so beautiful even in sleep
it makes the heart pound.
If those deep-lashed eyes should open—
ah, remember Semele.

Downstairs in the silent livingroom
sheer curtains have drawn up moonlight
into long straight bars of shade/less shade
imprisoning carpets, sofas, chairs.
Open the curtains, press fevered body
against the icy glass,
drink diamonds from lumined snow
let full moon flood in free
etherize this body back
into its own dark peace.

A Sunday Curse

On the drive out from the city
the FM station fades, and Handel's
Israel in Egypt is displaced
by Camrose—CFCW cowboys
with phony Texan drawls
announcing songs of love and tequila

A distant field is being harried
by a small but growing tornado.
I imagine this phenomenon
Is the sky's retribution
for unnatural waves sent through its air

0 you disk jockey,
you son-of-a-local-Swede
hiding behind your assumed name
and your microphone,
May this tornado pick you up
—and your pickup truck—
and slam you both to earth
in some real southwestern desert
And may you regain consciousness
to find a case of tequila beside you
shattered by hailstones for rain,
and fuelling fires, fires,
fires that run along the ground.

Violoncello

My abandoned 'cello leans away
into a dark basement corner
at the same angle it leaned into me:
I seldom practised it, it never forgave,
and always, when I picked it up
it bit me, its hard-edged ribs
digging into my legs
its sharp shoulders hard
against my breasts
its tuning pegs impertinent
in my left ear, my hair.
Clearly, we were not made for each other.
And yet I loved, love and will love it—
its sound that still wraps round me
even though I am not wrapped around it.

My first 'cello had a tricky endpin
that came out at odd times
like some mute exhibitionist.
But I won that round by
tightening its screw so it stayed out.
One day it proved effective
as a weapon of self-defence,
giving right through the soft leather vamp
of an amorous Spaniard's loafer.
As he ran roaring down the stairs
I called after him threatening
to complete his stigmata for Easter.

I'll likely never play again
and that has nothing to do
with my first boyfriend
who dropped me for a 'cellist, saying
she knew how to spread her her legs—and would.
What could I expect from a violinist?

The 'cello does not speak from its corner,
wrapped in its dark brown shroud,
dark leather belt around its soft middle,
dark leather collar around Modigliani neck,
the two metallic buttons glitter—
eyes of a soul gone mad from want of love.

Cactus Documentary

"Deep in the heart of the Negev desert,
the artichoke thrives."
Laughing, my son gets up from his homework
to close the window and shut out
the documentary on the neighbour's TV.
"That guy would watch anything," he scoffs.
The neighbour, an unkempt man with one arm
watches everything on TV
as well as everything he can see
through his uncurtained windows.
One night another neighbour reported him
standing nude in the middle of his kitchen
looking, she said, like a large pear on two toothpicks.
His boredom is broadcast but not in colour,
except on Friday nights, when the woman comes.
Their ritual has become intrusively familiar.
Television blares until midnight
then they become the entertainment,
their sounds carrying through all open windows:
"Get away from me, you animal!"
Slap!
"You slut! I paid good money for you!"
The prickly pear survives
by creating its own desert.

"Grief Like a Rock"

song by Mikis Theodorakis

The song goes on,
a tune played on bouzoukia
so happy it belies
its own burden
Grief is
not like a rock.
Is rock
rock not polished to reflect
ritual motions of unfelt sorrow
This is rough granite.
Out of this rock
tombstones are quarried—
rock, hung, inside the throat,
improbable
as sudden death
from vocal cords its weight
will stretch to breaking of
the voice to
a fractured whisper
escaping before the bosom
closes, and becomes
the pug-mill for the stones of soul.